AN

ADDRESS

IN BEHALF OF THE

Society for the Promotion of Collegiate and Theological Education at the West.

DELIVERED AT ITS TENTH ANNIVERSARY,
IN WORCESTER, MASSACHUSETTS, OCTOBER 26TH, 1853.

BY

REV. JOSEPH F. TUTTLE,
OF ROCKAWAY, N. J.

NEW-YORK:
JOHN F. TROW, PRINTER, 49 ANN STREET.
1854.

ADDRESS.

MR. PRESIDENT,

In rising to address this Society, I am embarrassed by recalling the distinguished names of those who have occupied this position in former years. Of this there is but one ground of complaint, and that is, the almost complete exhaustion of the materials for an occasion like this. The enthusiasm of your Corresponding Secretary in spreading before us those enlarged views of our "Great West," which thrill every attentive reader, has been caught by the men whom, from time to time, you have invited, to press those views on the convictions not merely of your Society but of the American Church.

When the idea of such a Society as this was first suggested, I was a student at Lane Seminary, having gone there as a graduate of Marietta College. I was present as a spectator during the sittings of that great convention of Western ministers in Cincinnati, which commenced June 9th, 1842. In some respects, it was one of the most important meetings, if not the most important ever held west of the Alleghanies. It was a critical period with the Calvinistic Churches at the West, when the few laborers, stout-hearted and trusting as they were, staggered under the responsibilities of a work whose magnitude was appalling and constantly increasing. They saw the flood of souls rolling in, as if the ocean itself had broken its bounds, and was spreading its tides of undying life over the vast areas of that goodly land. They well knew that flood could be arrested only by the hand that sent it, nor could they pray for such an event. The pioneers of our churches were there from the western slope of the Alleghanies, from the shores of Erie and Michigan lakes, from the banks of the Ohio, the Wabash, the Illinois, the Kentucky, the Mississippi, and the Missouri—from hill and prairie, to tell the common story of a great harvest, white for the reaper, with only here and there a sickle gathering in the precious sheaves. But what could they do—a few hundred laborers—in reaping a field like that which reached from the lakes to the mouth of the Ohio, from Independence on the Missouri to Marietta on the Ohio? To me it seemed a convention of heart-heavy men—to each of whom one might have said as King Artaxerxes did to Nehemiah, "Why is thy countenance sad, seeing thou art not sick? This is nothing else but sorrow of heart." And it *was* nothing else but sorrow of heart, for they could have said, "Thou hast brought a vine out of Egypt: thou hast cast out the heathen and planted it. Thou preparedst room before it, and didst cause it to take deep root, and it filled the land. The hills were covered with the shadow of it, and the boughs thereof were like the goodly cedars. She sent out her boughs unto the sea and her branches unto the river. Why hast thou broken down her hedges, so that all they which pass by the way do pluck her? The boar out of the wood doth waste, and the wild beast of the field doth devour it." As one looked on their anxious faces, and heard their tearful prayers, and was thrilled with their earnest tale of desolation, the fact itself making the eloquence of their appeals for help, the wondering spectator might have thought within himself, surely each of these men can use the language of Jeremiah, "His word was in my heart as a burning fire shut up in my bones, and I was weary with forbearing and I could not stay." With, perhaps, the single exception of the irrepressible pleasantries of Dr. Cox, the meeting was as sombre as death.

I give you merely my impressions. It may have struck others differently, but it seems hardly possible that such a body of practical and zealous Christians could have felt otherwise. One delegate stated that his Presbytery, with twelve ministers, covered nine large counties; another one, that his Presbytery, with ten ministers, covered nine counties; another still, that his Presbytery, with four ministers, extended over twelve counties of land rich as the valley of the Nile. Some stated that you might travel hundreds of miles, and yet only at vast intervals find an Evangelical church; and others, that ten, fifteen, and even thirty counties of glorious territory rapidly filling up, had not a single Evangelical church of any kind or description. All agreed that population was rushing in like tides in high latitudes, whilst the Evangelical ministry was increasing by additions almost imperceptible.

Among the topics discussed at large, were education for the ministry, Home Missions, Western Colleges and Theological Seminaries, relation between Presbyterianism and Congregationalism, and the necessity of a day of fasting, humiliation and prayer, for the outpouring of God's spirit on the churches.

I allude to these things as it were to lead you back to the very rock which was smitten with the rod of prayer, and forthwith gushed out a stream of water so pure, refreshing, and abundant, that it has made glad the city of our God. Here was the very place which was honored in starting a train of causes resulting in two of the grandest charities ever presented to the American Church, the providing an adequate ministry, and church extension. The originators of both these schemes were members of that convention.

In 1843, it was my good fortune to be present at a meeting of the Faculty of Marietta College, when your Corresponding Secretary was also present, and among other things he read a notable letter from my venerated theological instructor, Dr. Beecher,—(*sat magnos honores ei tribui non posse*)—and that letter left a deep impression on my mind. In another place I shall take the liberty of repeating a single paragraph. I was well acquainted with the condition of *that* college. I knew the officers and the trustees, and in my estimation, never was there a more devoted and earnest body of men associated to accomplish a worthy aim. They had prayerfully laid the foundations of that college on the Word of God, for the glory of Christ in furnishing a living, pious and learned ministry for the West. It was a choice spot, a very "Hill of Zion." Standing on the site of that college building, in one direction you could see the Beautiful River winding along its path of silver through one of the loveliest valleys in the world. In another direction you could detect the clear water of the Muskingum breaking through the hills which rose on either side. Down yonder, scarce a rifle-shot distant, is the very spot on which those noble colonists, under Gen. Rufus Putnam, left their clumsy boat, called by its builders "the Adventure Galley," but better named by its crew, the Mayflower, honored in carrying a freight in kind like that which consecrated the other Mayflower, a holy name for the good of all generations. Up yonder on the fine "second bottom" which slopes down to the Muskingum, is the site of the rude stockade fort, in which these men were obliged to find a refuge from the heathen around them, whom God afterwards cast out before them. There is the very spot on which the Rev. William Birck, "a New-England man," preached the first sermon to white men north of the Ohio. It was on "Sunday, the 20th of July, 1788," and his text was a worthy initiation of gospel preaching in the infant empire; "Now therefore, if ye will obey my voice indeed, and keep my covenant, then ye shall be a peculiar treasure unto me above all people; for all the earth is mine, and ye shall be unto me a kingdom of priests and a holy nation." (*Exodus* xix., 5, 6.) In another direction you see the venerable church, erected on a spot set apart for evangelical worship of the Triune God. And then, too, you see mounds and fortifications of some race which has passed away, not leaving even a dim tradition to tell who they were, whence they came, and whither they have gone.

This town of Marietta, I repeat it, is a choice spot; and here it was that good men planted a college, not to realize fortunes by it, but to furnish gospel ministers to the Great West. But at the time of the convention of western ministers at Cincinnati, in 1842, the enterprise was passing through a most fiery ordeal. Its founders had borne heavy burdens until "every shoulder was peeled." They were in debt, and every step in advance was increasing the burden. There were young men who longed for an education, but their purses, collapsed into the emptiness of poverty, were poor paymasters for an enterprise so costly. And yet shall they be sent back to the plough and workshop when the demand for ministers was so urgent? And here too was a faculty of professors, fully accomplished in their separate departments, admired by the community, venerated by their pupils, and constantly invited to lucrative posts in other places, and yet content to stay by the college, as a parent by a darling child, although their salaries at best were small, and not very promptly paid at that. Shall that faculty be disbanded, those young men sent home, and those consecrated halls be closed? Would God that some of our rich Christians with their dangerous plethora of money, might have been there to have had these tremendous questions rolled on their consciences by the Great Head of the Church! They could not have "passed by on the other side."

I never think of that faculty but with most profound admiration for their steady sacrifice of themselves on the altar of Christian letters for the glory of Christ. And even they could not have done what they did, had not the trustees of the college been men of faith. Young, thriving, energetic, business men, they had been filled with a heavenly ardor for the Saviour of sinners, by whose grace they had been "born again" a short time previous to the founding of the college, as if to carry that very enterprise on their shoulders; they were troubled on every side, yet not distressed; perplexed, but not in despair; cast down, but not destroyed. They never wavered for a moment, whilst making almost superhuman efforts to place the institution they loved so dearly above the fear of the "hungry ruin" that stared them in the face.

Mr. President, you may think me warm in my enthusiasm, but you will pardon a son for expatiating somewhat zealously on the virtues of the mother that bore him. I love my *alma mater*, and she always shall be cherished in an honored place in my heart's affections. When I think of that dark, almost desperate period, from 1842 to 1845, when it would not have been a surprising event, if at any moment Marietta College had dashed on the rocks, I recall the names of her Faculty and her Board of Trustees with an irrepressible and loving admiration.

But let me not be understood to ignore the worth and the trials of the other colleges, at Hudson, Crawfordsville, and Jacksonville. I speak of Marietta, because I was an eye-witness to the difficulties there encountered; but could some eye-witnesses from each of these colleges here testify, they would declare to you that I have not exaggerated the difficulties which frowned on these institutions, and the self-sacrificing devotion with which their friends met these difficulties.

It was at this period of darkness that might be felt, that the voice of Providence almost articulate, was heard saying, "Fear ye not, *stand still* and see the salvation of the Lord." And yet in one of those blessed paradoxes, which so beautifully blend the human instrumentality with the Divine efficiency, the same voice was heard, saying, "Wherefore criest thou unto *me?* Speak unto them that *they go forward.*" And it was on this wise. "In the month of June, 1842, a Convention of Western Churches was held at Cincinnati, and at that Convention the critical condition of institutions of learning at the West, came under consideration. The idea afterward occurred to a member of this Convention, of uniting under one head the several agencies of those institutions, which had been operating upon the eastern field. It was subsequently ascertained that a similar idea had occurred to an eastern agent as well as to a distinguished pastor of an eastern church. In the providence of God, these minds were brought together, and through a period of six months the subject was discussed in private circles from the Atlantic to the Mississippi, (Per. Doc. West. Coll. Society.)

It was during this period of discussion that Dr. Beecher wrote the letter to which allusion has already been made. In that letter, after describing various meetings which had been held to prepare the way for the organization of this Society, and some formidable obstacles which had been overcome, the Doctor says: "There can be no doubt the cause is popular. Bacon, of New Haven, and others, said at the close of the New-York meeting, this is the most important thing we have done, the best link in the chain of moral causes, the most powerful citadel of defence against foreign aggression and internal dissensions—a new era, when the importance of evangelical colleges shall be appreciated, not only by men of literary and far-reaching minds, but by the whole church of God as a primary object of her prayers and charities. Is it not the Lord's doings? The rising of a new sun on the bosom of a dark cloud passing away?"

Such were the harbingers which heralded in the organization of this society, and the deep interest which circumstances gave this event in my mind will be my apology for dwelling on it at such length.

Mr. President, what I intended to condense in a paragraph, has unconsciously grown into a speech, and yet I have not touched some thoughts which seem to me to be in point on such an occasion as this.

With more trepidation than vanity, we may say we belong to a great nation, with an extraordinary destiny of some sort in prospect. Our institutions, if we except the local one of involuntary bondage, are the very opposite of the monstrous feudalism of the old world. Here, in a most important sense, a man *is* a man. He can purchase and hold the soil. Every avenue to the highest preferments is open to him. The serf of the old world becomes the citizen of the new, and it is no wonder that when this broad land, from the Atlantic to the Pacific, a right imperial domain, was thrown open with the most generous hospitality to the oppressed of the world, they moved hither as by a common impulse. Our resources are of the amplest dimensions and of the most numerous varieties. We have almost every sort of minerals in abundance, from the magnetic ores of New Jersey to the gold dust of California. We have prairies and plains, a vast expanse, well nigh sufficient to bread the world. The amazing resources of the West have only begun their development. Such a land is probably not to be named on our globe. Our progress has been like the works of nature here, astonishingly great. From the unprotected helplessness of Jamestown and Plymouth Rock, we have grown to twenty-five millions of souls, and from a few weak colonies, scarce able to repel the attacks of savages, we are become thirty-one sovereign commonwealths and four territories, each possessed of immense means for the arts and enjoyments of peace or the necessities of war. And these are associated in one central government of such might, that the empires of the old world holds us in no small fear.

Our nation is great in its enterprise. The ingenuity of our mechanics has passed into a proverb. Our locomotives are not unknown in England, and they drag the imperial car from St. Petersburgh to Moscow. Our genius is at work in every cotton-gin in the East Indies and Africa. Our agricultural implements at the World's Fair in London excited universal admiration. In fact, it would seem as if our countrymen can make anything, from a wooden clock to the simplest, speediest, and surest printing press. As to commerce, we are the peer of Great Britain, and our sailors have no superiors, their consummate skill and boldness eliciting common applause, whether exhibited in a yacht race or in battling with icebergs in the north seas. At home our energy is the supplement of that abroad. We dam our creeks and rivers, and as by magic towns and cities start up in the wilderness, and the hum of machinery is heard, where but a little while ago the wolf howled. We dig down or through mountains, fill up the valleys, hang the slight but strong bridge over the yawning abysses, for those iron roads which bind all parts of this country together.

But this is a trifle in comparison with our growth as a nation, especially at the West. Only sixty-six years have passed away since Putnam landed at Marietta, and now Ohio is the third State in point of power. Judge Burnet, who has just died, found Cincinnati a cluster of huts in 1796, and now it has in and about not less than 150,000 souls. Cleveland, Zanesville, Dayton, Columbus, Louisville, Indianapolis, Madison, Alton, Chicago, St. Louis, Iowa City, Milwaukie, Jamestown, Detroit, Saginaw, St. Pauls, and hundreds of smaller towns have grown up as in a night. Scarcely has one State been admitted into the Union, ere another is at the door. How they have gathered force, with the speed of a descending avalanche! A few days more and Minnesota and Nebraska will be imitating the sovereignty of Iowa and Wisconsin. The wave rushes on unchecked. The wild man and the buffalo are vanishing, and soon the locomotive will be uttering its scream of triumph as it whirls its way across the Rocky Mountains. The field on this side of that range is soon to be occupied with States. It is a "manifest destiny," or rather a resistless decree from the God of Providence. Those vast solitudes are to be peopled by men sheltered beneath the American flag. And Utah, midway between the Pacific and the Mississippi, what are we to do with *it?* Shall it be admitted, and its High Priests establish their seraglios at Washington? Here is a knotty problem; how shall we solve it? And beyond that is the strangest, strongest, and I had almost said, the wickedest commonwealth on the continent, agitated as with earthquake passions.

Mr. President, this *is* a great nation, and we have more reason to utter this word with alarm than with vanity. It is a fearfully thrilling sight to see a single horse running at a furious speed beyond the control of his driver, but it is not so thrilling as to see a crowded train of cars dashing like lightning along the iron railway, when you know that the displacement of a rail, the breaking of an axle, or the mistake of a signal at the drawbridge, may hurry a multitude into eternity in the twinkling of an eye. The world at large is not greatly affected by the revolutions and counter-revolutions of Buenos Ayres and Chili, but this nation has woven its destiny among those of the first class nations of the earth, and the speed with which we are rushing on to greatness is one most fearful to behold.

Our dangers are as great as our blessings, and they come in every wave of population which breaks upon our shores. The religious element of the people by no means keeps pace with growing wickedness. Our great cities often resound with the clangor of martial music on the Sabbath at burials and the laying of corner stones. An insidious and wide-spread conspiracy is digging away the foundations of the Christian Sabbath, to convert it into a mere gala day as at Paris and Rome. A powerful association of learned and wicked men is engaged in inoculating our nation with German infidelity, and the virus is already showing the malignity of a fatal disease. The Papacy is bringing all its ingenious devices, backed up with abundant pecuniary means, to give America the despotism of Hildebrand and the impiety of Leo X., and already we have the fooleries which have made Spain, Mexico, and Italy emasculate, stuck up at every corner and adored in every community. Hegel and Tom Paine, Joe Smith and John Hughes, seem one in a common purpose to root out the chosen seeds of truth which the Mayflower conveyed hither, and which have already brought forth some an hundred fold, some sixty, some thirty. These infidels are working with tremendous zeal, and it is to be feared with much success.

Irreligion, or rather *no religion*, if you will pardon the paradox, is increasing, and hundreds of thousands among us neither fear God nor regard man. Intemperance is increasing like the deluge, and I see but one Noah's ark upon the waters. It comes from north-east. Involuntary slavery is tearing away our heart-strings, invoking on us the wrath of heaven and embroiling us in civil feuds and bloodshed.

Without a parallel our nation is great in the besetting dangers of the present day, and if we perish it will not be like the fall of Babylon or Rome, or Mexico, but a greater fall than that, fraught with infinite sorrow to us and our children and to the millions of oppressed in other lands whose eyes are turned to us with the yearnings and longings of hearts sick with hope deferred. The day of our fall, if there be such a day, will be a sad one in the annals of time. A wail shall go up from the appalled nations, "Alas! that great nation that was clothed in fine linen, and purple, and scarlet, and decked with gold and precious stones and pearls: for in one hour so great riches is come to nought!" Whilst a mighty voice shall sound through the earth, "Rejoice over her, thou heaven, and ye holy apostles and prophets, for God hath avenged you on her!"

But if so be God save us and make us a peculiar nation, then may the world say in truth, "And what one nation in the earth is like this thy people!"

Mr. President, if you will refer to the permanent documents of your society, you will perceive that I do not take for granted a fact not demonstrated, viz., that *the chief instrumentality for evangelizing this great land, is the preaching of Jesus Christ and him crucified, foolishness indeed in the estimation of some, a stumbling block to others, but owned of heaven as the power of God and the wisdom of God.* If our nation is to be saved from threatened ruin, from infidelity, from popery, from irreligion, it will not be by the mere circulation of even such a heavenly literature as the American Tract Society is giving to our nation, nor by the indefinite multiplication of Bibles and Testaments. In their place in the great system of means these societies are doing a work of great moment, and we cannot press that work with too much energy. But books cannot do the work of living men. God sometimes uses one of these blessed pages to plant the seed of grace in some heart, but the great mass of converts are reached by the voice of the living preacher. It was a living ministry that our Lord sent out to preach, to call men to repentance, even as living messengers, and not written letters, were sent from heaven to sound the good news of a Saviour born which is Christ the Lord. It was this instrumentality which set the world in a blaze when the persecution scattered the disciples from Jerusalem. It was this which rocked the papal throne when Luther's lion voice preached to thrilled multitudes the doctrine of justification by faith. It was this which shook Scotland to its centre, when John Knox held forth the word of life. It was this which reached the hearts of the grim colliers of Kingswood, when Charles Wesley told them of Christ; which held acres of human beings rivetted and spell-bound, whilst Whitfield proclaimed the gospel; and which caused men and women to swoon with terror, as Edwards at Northampton spoke with angel utterance of "Sinners in the hands of an angry God."

I cannot stop to prove it, but must take for granted, that our chief want is a living ministry, learned, pious, zealous, and in sufficient numbers. Give us this instrumentality and all others will follow as a matter of necessity.

There is still another point, on which I must beg your indulgence a few moments, viz., that the supply of ministers is not at all in proportion to the urgent demands of a work which is increasing on our hands with frightful rapidity. The language of the General Assembly at Buffalo, in May last, is but the note which indicates a sorrow common to the whole Calvinistic family. In their narrative they tell us, there is "one topic on which a very large number of our Presbyteries, and especially in the great Western field, dwell with earnest and mournful emphasis. It is the destitution of ministers, the utter inadequacy of the laborers to the vast work that is to be done." Diffuse their labors as they may, they tell us of many churches which have no one to break to them the bread of life; and of destitutions, to obtain a supply for which their utmost efforts are unavailing. The cry is sent up to us from every quarter of the land, "come over and help us." And it is because that cry has been so long sounding in vain, that despondency and gloom overshadow many a field of promise, and oppress many a heart that responds to the sympathies of the Gospel. To add to the oppressiveness of this despondency, the future seems darker and more forbidding than the present. The candidates for the ministry which our Presbyteries report, are few in number. The broad and open avenues to wealth and higher objects of ambition are crowded with eager competitors; and among them not a few who have professedly consecrated their talents to the God of their salvation. The self-denying path to the ministry * * * has but here and there a youthful traveller. If there is any one feature of our present state that should humble us as an Assembly, and the churches under our care, before God, this is one. In 1849 the old school Board of Education, say, what I think, in substance, they have repeated each subsequent year: "The Board deem it their duty to keep steadily before the Assembly the alarming and humiliating fact that the number of candidates for the ministry of our church, is, at best, but stationary." The Albany Convention of Congregational Ministers, one year ago, spoke of the "alarming disproportion between the increase of our population, and the increase of the ministers of the Gospel."

Mr. President and Christian friends, there is the sting of mingled truth and falsehood in the sarcasm of the shrewdest and most to be dreaded enemy the Gospel has in this country—I mean Archbishop Hughes, when he said, "Nearly the whole class by which the Protestant ministry was formerly supplied, has disappeared altogether; and although they have places and pensions in theological seminaries, they cannot find candidates to accept them, although they have education and position offered to them; *the race of pious young men, as they used to be called twenty years ago, has died out, and this fact is acknowledged. They know not what is to be the consequence, if Providence should not raise up candidates to continue their ministry.*" Our wily foe has discovered the lock of our strength, and he was not shrewd enough to suppress a sarcasm, which from his lips makes a thrilling appeal to us. The living ministry, as an instrument, is *chief* and *vital*, and in this we are faltering. We are building churches in all shapes, grotesque and beautiful, from a cross to a circle, with all kinds of steeples, and with all sorts of approximations to the gorgeous mockeries of the middle ages; we are pointing to this and that spacious and costly palace in which our merchant princes have "settled on their lees;" we name with a boast this and that and the other distinguished son of the church, who have attained the high places of power; we educate by our example and precepts the baptized children of the church into an exaggerated estimate of the blessedness of "heaping up riches;" we talk complacently of our glorious "pilgrim fathers," the wealth and importance of "our church," the munificence of our home and foreign charities; we grow eloquent over the respectability, intelligence and commanding influence of our communions; instead of facing the tremendous fact that the chief instrumentality which has raised us to our present position, and has achieved our past victories, an instrumentality which has employed the sanctified energies of such as the Mathers, the two

Edwards, Hopkins, Whitfield, Witherspoon, the Tennants, and Samuel Davies; I say, instead of facing the tremendous fact that this instrumentality is now patronised and blessed in a measure but little more than sufficient to hold the ground we now have, whilst for the great world of the West it is as inadequate as the sickle of a single reaper to gather the harvests of the Genesee.

Did the limits assigned me in this address permit, I would like to dwell on two points which can only be suggested, viz., (1.) Christian parents in great part hold the remedy for this lamentable state of things. Could the same means be introduced into the nursery and family that gave Samuel, Timothy, and Doddridge, to the special work of God's ambassadors, a revolution would soon be apparent, and (2.) the effect of a general revival of genuine religion through our churches on replenishing the ranks of the ministry. A very large proportion of the ministers now in the field were converted in the pentecostal revivings which distilled their influences so mightily on the churches twenty years ago.

But these points I must omit and ask your attention to another point of vast importance—I mean *the establishment and endowment of Christian schools and colleges.* In my estimation, your society, Mr. President, has grasped the great educational idea of the age—the very idea with which one is to chase a thousand and two put ten thousand to flight. I know not how it may be in New England, but in the Middle and Western States I have noticed extreme reluctance on the part of young men to become beneficiaries on the lists of our educational societies, and in speaking this impression, I do not wish to utter a word in disparagement of those societies. They have done, and are yet doing a great work, and yet there are young men of talents and piety who refuse aid coming in that way. Many who have received the aid look back with regret, because the obnoxious odium of a poor charity student clings to them like pitch, and is often suggested to their memory in a way not at all pleasant. In a sense, every boy in the free-schools of Boston and New-York is a charity scholar, and yet when one of these passes from the high school to the active business of life, he does it without a taint which would make him blush to recall "his antecedents." In these institutions the sons of the coal-heaver and street-sweep sit side by side with the sons of the merchant prince, and the gifted civilian pursuing the same studies, sustained by the same bounty and aspiring after the same honors.

In a more restricted sense, this fact holds good of the military and naval academies at West Point and Annapolis. The son of the senator cannot say to the son of the straitened backwoodsman, "you are a charity scholar!" There is a common level of privilege on which they all stand, in theory at least, merit being the only means of rank. In this fact I see an idea which I would might be wrought out in practice, at *least in one model Christian college. I should like* to see a college of the church so amply endowed and allowed to expend its income so judiciously that all the students within its walls, without regard to the wealth or poverty of their parents, would receive all its privileges free. Its instruction, its rooms, its libraries, and its scholarships ample for the encouragement of virtuous industry, and small enough to act as a spur to indolence, all should be free to those whose merits entitled them to the foundation. I verily believe the change would be most beneficial on the interests of learning, and especially on the ministry. And were I a rich man, with the same feelings which now possess me, I would not let a year pass without trying the scheme on some one of our Western Colleges. I cannot now see a way in which a Christian philanthropist could make such a permanent and glorious investment of money, lucrative in the dividends of eternity, as to endow a college in some such way. If I mistake not the drift of things, this idea in substance, but no doubt modified by wisdom and experience, is beginning to "possess the reins" of this society, and this now rises up before me as the grandest educational idea of the Christian Church.

But an objection is raised, the very one which has made education societies a stench in the nostrils of some excellent Christians and churches, viz.: *that many will receive the benefits of these funds of the church who will not preach the gospel.* That this has been the case with educational funds I do not question, nay, I know such to have been the case in some instances. And yet it seems to me to be an unworthy contraction of the schemes and plans which the Church should devise for the accomplishment of the grandest idea she can conceive, that of giving to the West and to the World an adequate ministry. In the mountains of New-Jersey, capitalists blast at great expense and fling away hundreds of tons of rock, and find their compensation in the rich ore which they by this means reach. One of my neighbors, an earnest, sensible laborer, visited the gulches of California to find gold, and he has told me that he was obliged to move a mass of common earth and rock at a large expense of time, money, and fatigue, but he knew he must do it in order to reach the precious metal thus buried. A short time since he came back with his pockets full of money, and I have never heard him utter a complaint that he had to shovel up so much base dirt! The gold he got at by the means, was his reward.

And why should not the Church be as wise in her search after the hid treasures of good ministers as these men digging for iron or gold? Suppose you do have a hundred men in your catalogue, fifty of whom, more intelligent than when you took them, fall back into the private pursuits of life, are you right certain that you have not done a deed which shall elevate the intelligence and efficiency of your churches, and open sources of Christian activity and charity which otherwise might have been as closely sealed as the rock before Moses smote it? Let me farther suppose, that of the remaining fifty ten become lawyers, and ten physicians, the rest holding forth the word of life in the pulpit. Will you say the Church has lost its investment because those lawyers and physicians did not study theology? Go into any of our prominent churches and towns, and tell me whether you cannot find some pious physicians and lawyers that the Church and community could ill afford to lose, men whose influence is so commanding and good, that rather than do without it, the Church could have well afforded to be at the sole expense of their education? I can name church after church blessed with such educated men, and I rejoice in God when I see him adding to the substantial energies of the Christian Church by giving such men the heart and means to educate themselves, although it be not to preach. To put such men in such positions would be no more a waste of the Church's funds than to cast seed into the soil to yield a harvest in return. It would be a wise economy in the end.

I will take the most extreme view of the case, and assert that if out of the hundred men whom your bountiful provisions have called together, ninety-nine disappoint you, and yet the hundredth one proves to be an Elias Cornelius, a William Goodell, or a James Richards, the Church ought to consider the return as ample as the gold-digger who has toiled day after day, removing load after load of refuse dirt, but at last comes to an ingot mass of pure gold. But such a number of young men will produce many more laborers than one, and I do believe that our Christian Colleges should be so endowed that a very large number of youth and young men might be induced to enter their halls, out of which the Holy Ghost should call the special messengers of the cross. And looking back over the field of my own personal observation, and comparing it with the striking tables compiled by Prof. Tyler of Amherst, showing how many who are now preaching Christ were converted in College, I would not always forbid these privileges of free Christian Colleges to impenitent youth, whose morals are good and whose talents are promising.

Mr. President, I do not wish to compromise your Society by these remarks. To some they may appear quixotic and extreme, and no one is responsible for them but myself, but I do think that next to home religion, like that of Hannah, Eunice, and Doddridge's mother, and such great refreshings of the Church at large, as were once enjoyed in this country, the great means of furnishing an adequate ministry to the West, and the world, is found in an enlarged system of free Christian Colleges, out of which may be selected the ambassadors who shall beseech men to be reconciled to God.

Thousands rejoice in what your Society has done and is

now doing. Let your motto be "*excelsior*" or if that appear too secular, then inscribe on your banner, "Not as though I had already attained, either were already made perfect, * * * but this one thing I do, forgetting those things which are behind and reaching forth unto those things which are before, I press toward the mark for the prize of the high calling of God in Christ Jesus."

www.ingramcontent.com/pod-product-compliance
Lightning Source LLC
LaVergne TN
LVHW020634110826
845149LV00004B/1190

* 9 7 8 1 4 1 8 1 9 0 9 9 6 *